THE
Old Photographs
SERIES

ROSS-ON-WYE

At this stage, no speed limit was needed on the Hereford Road travelling through Fownhope. The residents of Ferry Road don their Sunday best, c.1910.

THE
Old Photographs
SERIES

ROSS-ON-WYE

Compiled by
Tom Rigby & Alan Sutton

**ALAN
SUTTON**

BATH • AUGUSTA • RENNES

First Published 1994
© Copyright Tom Rigby and Alan Sutton

Alan Sutton Limited
12 Riverside Court
Bath BA2 3DZ

ISBN 0 7524 0002 9

Typesetting & origination by
Alan Sutton Limited
Printed in Great Britain

Aerial view of the town.

Contents

Gathering in the hay in the 1920s was a laborious task and very much a community effort. There were no machines to help and, as the photograph shows, this group are using wooden hay-rakes.

Introduction

High on a sandstone cliff, overlooking a large loop in the beautiful River Wye, lies the historic market town of Ross-on-Wye. An attractive and friendly town.

Ross has long been promoted by tourist organisations as the 'Gateway of the Wye Valley', an apt description, for after meandering through miles of rich Herefordshire farmland, the river moves into a more dramatic setting below Ross. The wooded slopes of Coppet Hill, the Doward on one side and the Forest of Dean plateau on the other, sweep down to the banks bringing to Vaga, the river's Roman name, an air of almost magical beauty.

Recently, one of the area's best-known residents, Sir John Harvey-Jones, referred to the town by an even more compelling title, 'The Jewels of the Wye'. The pastureland that surrounds it has the rich green of emeralds, harvest-time brings the gold of the grain and fruit, the soil and buildings have the redness of garnet, and the river has its diamonds sparkling in the summer sun.

To complement this jewelbox of nature, man has built buildings that catch the eye of the architect but also delight those with a less specialized knowledge. The parish church of St Mary, with its narrow spire, provides a landmark over many miles, and the Market House built of red sandstone has, for over three centuries, intrigued the visitor with its design, a style associated more with Latin parts of the world than a town on the borders of Wales. Although the church and Market House catch the attention of the tourist, Ross has many more tales to tell, hidden in its alleyways and quaint buildings that have resisted the change of the twentieth century. There have of course been changes. It would not have been in the interests of those living and working in the town, if developments had not kept pace with the world and new technology of the last twenty to thirty years.

The panorama of tall buildings and narrow streets has not altered significantly in the last 100 years but at ground level one becomes aware that sadly but inevitably the supermarkets have caused the disappearance of many small family-run shops. Also gone since the Second World War are the brewery, the flour mill and the railways. At the moment, the car reigns supreme, little headway having been made with schemes of pedestrianization. The building of fast roads to speed the traffic between the Midlands and South Wales has cut swathes through meadowland and has had a profound influence on the town. Ross-on-Wye is not just a place for retirement or the holidaymaker but has become a valuable centre for those whose business takes them over wide tracts of Wales and the western half of England.

This fascinating collection of old photographs of Ross gives us a wonderful opportunity to see not only how the town and its inhabitants have changed in appearance over the last one hundred years or so but also, conversely, how little changed are some others. The book is a nostalgic journey that all who know Ross will enjoy.

Martin Morris MBE
Ross-on-Wye
April 1994

Acknowledgements

My thanks go to all those who have kindly lent photographs and postcards that have been included in this book. In particular, the contribution from Mr Martin Morris MBE was invaluable, and without his knowledge of the town and its people, this book would still be at the research stage. I must also mention the contribution of the late Mr. R.E. Davies whose wonderful collection of photographs appear in this book.

My special thanks also go to Mr R.H.Roff, Kevin Minton of the Ross Gazette, Mr John Coombes, Tom Passey, Tim Ward, Joan Ollis and Harry Ruston.

One
Community Spirit

A display by Ross gymnasts.

ROSS-ON-WYE CELEBRITIES AS SEEN BY "MATT"

A few of the leading personalities of Ross-on-Wye pictured by "Matt," our caricaturist, during his recent visit to the famous Herefordshire town.

10

His immaculate military bearing made John Preedy an impressive Bandmaster of the Ross Town Band in the years following its revival in 1924.

Elections have always bought zip to local life. Conservative candidate Mr Roberts is seen here being enthusiastically received by people of all ages in the 1920s, although the dog at the bottom of the picture doesn't seem too interested.

A group pictured outside the offices of auctioneers Cooper & Preece during the County Council Election campaign of 1907.

An enlargement from the previous photograph shows more detail of the posters.

Pupils from Walford School, looking attentive (well, some of them) during a chemistry lesson, c.1925.

Radio presenter and celebrity Jimmy Young entertains some of the local female population during a charity gala in 1964.

Bob Webb, Chairman of Ross-on-Wye Urban Council, admires Mrs Rattray's telegram from the Queen, as she celebrates her 100th birthday on 15th July 1963.

Hereford's prospective Labour Parliamentary candidate, Tom Locksley is welcomed by Harold Davies, Labour MP for Leek in Staffordshire. The onlookers are (from left to right): Lawrence Riches; Ross's first Labour Councillor; Bill Welsh, Riches' successor; and A.R. Reynolds, Secretary of the constituency.

Major David Gibson-Watt (second from right), MP from 1956-74, in conversation with colleagues at the Conservative Club: Mr A.O. Hewitt, President of the Club (second from left); Bert Porter, Club Chairman (left); and Don Lowe, Secretary.

The name of this little girl is not known but she certainly does make a beautiful picture.

A seventeenth century engraving of John Kyrle (1637-1724), known locally as the 'Man of Ross' (first bestowed on him by the poet Alexander Pope). He lived opposite the Market Hall, in what are now the offices of the *Ross Gazette*, and was largely responsible for the early prosperity of the town. His generosity towards the needy, infirm and to those who generally sought his advice or help was realised when the entire population of Ross attended his funeral in November 1724. In 1924 the town donated the clock on the church tower as a memorial. Here, he is shown handing out money to the poor.

Mrs Margaret Shepherd (later to become a Dame) outside Buckingham Palace after receiving an OBE. With her are husband Mr T.C.R. Shepherd MBE, and their sons, one of whom, Colin, was later to became a local MP.

Mr and Mrs Salmon celebrate their Golden Wedding Anniversary with their family on 29th September 1962.

The Swiss Bazaar, held at Ross Congregational Church in 1890.

The boys and girls that made up the temperance organization, Band of Hope.

Another year, another carnival.

Improvization and imagination! A gondola is built onto a motorcycle sidecar for a procession during the annual town carnival in 1930.

Headmaster of Ross Senior Council School between the wars, Bernard Abel, and his wife, who was senior mistress, loved to put on costumed productions. In this picture, taken in the school playground at Cantilupe Road in March of 1926, they are directing the boys and girls in 'The Magic Fan.' The library now stands on the original site.

A picture of the Green family taken in the 1930s.

A fancy dress contest held at the Marsh to celebrate the Golden Jubilee in 1887.

Mr Roberts (and young assistant) at his plant nursery in Ross.

The opening of the Robert Ashley Memorial Hall at Walford in 1969. From left to right are: Major J.S.B. Gaskell; Mr Ted Allen (Secretary); Mr Handley (Headteacher at Walford School); and Mr W. Chinn.

The top table at the Ross Womens Union function, held at the Old Conservative Hall. From left to right are: Mrs Maude Kittle; Dame Margaret Shepherd; Mrs Eve Porter; and Mrs Dunlop.

The Ross branch of the National Farmers Union celebrates its Diamond Jubilee in 1969. From left to right are: Ernest Whittle; Jim Like (Secretary); -?-; George Johnson (County Secretary); -?-; -?-; Mr F. D. Oakley (Chairman); -?-; and Mr Hackett.

Council Chairman Bernard Hackett presents George Hardy with a certificate, upon his retirement as a surveyor, architect and public health inspector for the council in 1962.

Dib-dib... The Ross Cubs group pose for a photo at the old headquarters. Akele, John Constance, stands on the far right.

A wedding photograph taken during the 1920s.

The people in this family photograph are unknown, but the picture was taken at the turn of the century.

Mr Bert Baynham, Chairman of the Ross branch of the British Legion, lays a wreath at the foot of the memorial. Town reporter Martin Morris (far left) looks on.

'Wear your poppy with pride'. Mrs R.E. Davies and Cyril Burrows (whose father was at one time Governor of Bengal) stand in the doorway of the *Gazette* and collect on behalf of those who fought in the First and Second World Wars, c.1969.

The annual Rememberance Day service at the Prospect in 1962. Prebendary Gilbert Stockley presides.

Alarming Earthquake Shock.

The following appeared in our second edition only, last week.

Between half-past 5 and 25 minutes to 6 this (Thursday) morning a severe shock of earthquake was felt in Ross.

It is at present not possible to tell the precise direction of the earth wave; some people thinking it passed from east to west, and others from south to north.

Those who were awake in their beds at the time describe the sensation as that of a huge animal shaking itself, and others as if something under the bed caused an upheaval, making it rock more or less severely. In some cases bells were set ringing, and articles on tables, drawers, dressers, and mantel-pieces were made to jangle, and in some cases to fall down. We know of one case where a timepiece was stopped by the oscillation, and thus denoted the precise time it happened.

The consternation and alarm it caused in every house by the shock, operated very severely on people of a sensitive and nervous temperament, many having been rendered quite ill through it.

Some of the details which have reached us as to the damage done by the shock are the injury of several chimneys in the town, one of which, next the Post Office, has had a portion of the upper part shaken off, but this is partly due to faulty construction. Another has fallen at Sellack Marsh; and at Hereford similar accidents have befallen chimneys, notably two at the railway station, at which place a wall has also fallen. The pinnacles of two of the churches and the Cathedral have also been damaged.

We have received information from Weston-under-Penyard, Bromsash, and other places, of damage done to chimney stacks and old buildings.

Mr. C. H. Hall, of Ross, informs us that in a conversation he had had this morning with the guard of the mail train going from the west to the north, he told him that he thought when the shock struck the train between Hereford and Shrewsbury, that the carriages were off the line.

A day never to be forgotten! Ross-on-Wye experiences its first and thankfully to date, its last earthquake. This report appeared in the *Gazette* following the earth tremor which hit the town early on the morning of Thursday December 17th 1896 — and look at how little it got in the way of coverage!

A scene from Gilbert and Sullivan's 'Trial by Jury', staged by the Ross Operatic & Dramatic Society.

Just part of the entertainment during the Ross Carnival of 1888.

A family snapshot from the early part of this century.

This photograph of Evan, Nancy and Bernard Davall enjoying a day out on their motocycles was taken at Upton Bishop in the early 1920s.

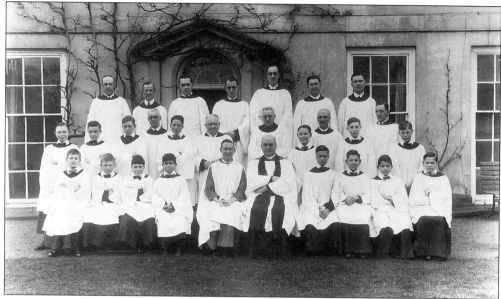

Ross Parish Church choir, pictured in front of the old Rectory on March 11th 1934. In the centre of the front row is Frederick Parsons, organist and choirmaster, who was also the town's weatherman for 60 years. The Rector, Reverend Beattie, was the father of Stephen Beattie, who was awarded the Victoria Cross for his gallantry in the St Nazaire raid of 1942.

In July 1991, during the last weeks of nearly 44 years as a reporter on the Ross Gazette, Martin Morris met the heroes of the Gulf War, while they were on a surprise visit to Goodrich Castle. In the centre is General 'Stormin' Norman Schwarzkopf, Commander in Chief of the allied forces in the Gulf and on the right is General Sir Peter de la Billiere, Commander of the British land forces.

The Queen and Prince Philip received a huge welcome from the thousands who had packed the Market Place, when they made a brief visit to Ross at the end of a day-long tour of Herefordshire in April 1957.

The fashion of the time!

The 1969 Bridstow Table-Tennis Marathon.

The Ross Choral Society provides an evening's entertainment for the local people.

The final meeting of the Ross and Whitchurch Rural Council in 1974.

The caption on the front of this photograph reads: 'These five badgers were dug out of one earth by five men with two dogs, and killed in one hour and twenty minutes on January 24th 1913. Three sows, weight: 26, 24 and 22 lbs. Two hogs, weight: 25lb each.'

Two

About Town

This picture, taken in Gloucester Road, gives an idea of the chaotic conditions drivers had to overcome in the 1950s before the building of the M50 and the bypass.

Alton Court pictured in the early years of this century.

Here are two views of Broad Street, one at the turn of the century and the other in the mid-1930s. See how little had changed.

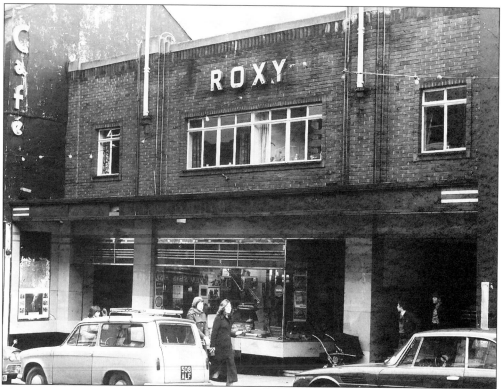

The Roxy Cinema, once a focal point for the town's youth. The Maltings shopping centre now stands in its place.

The black and white frontage (not genuine Tudor) of the Valley Hotel in Edde Cross Street disappeared when it was converted into flats on the present Rothsay Court.

Broad Street, once famed for its taverns, pictured in 1956.

A birds-eye view of the town from the top of the church tower.

A view of the town from the 'Horse Shoe Bend', with the spire of St Marys and the Royal Hotel standing prominently on top of the hill, c.1910.

The old Cattle Market at Homs Road. It stood here for over 100 years before it was moved to Over Ross in the late 1980s.

Aug 1910 Herefordshire.

Henry Dowell & Son, Launch and Boat Builders and Proprietors, Wyeside, Ross-on-Wye.

Launch and boat builder, proprietor, landlord of the Hope and Anchor Inn and owner of the paddle steamer *'Wilton Castle'*, Mr Henry Dowell, advertises his services in August of 1910.

Looking down Broad Street from the Market House, *c*.1900.

A pony and trap stop for a break outside the Swan Hotel, *c.*1910.

Looking up Gloucester Road during the early 1900s.

Broad Street in 1908.

Ten years or so after the demolition of the George Hotel, large scale redevelopment began on the other side of the Market Place. Raynor's drapery store is seen here shortly before the builders moved in.

'Dump your scrap metal here'. A campaign set up during the Second World War to utilise all sorts of scrap metal in the town and turn it into vital machinery and weapons, c.1943.

The Lover's Seat.
John Kyrles' Walk.

The Lover's Seat is a stile found on the tracks of the John Kyrle Walk which tours around the sights of the town and its surrounding countryside. Many stories exist about the origins of its name, one of which describes the plight of two young lovers, forbidden to see one another by their respective fathers. Tradition has it that they would meet at this point at midnight and share the only time they were able to meet gazing up at the stars.

Colinton, pictured at the turn of the century.

Broad Street in the late 1920s.

For an ancient town, Ross has surprisingly few half-timbered houses, but a fine example can be seen in High Street. Formerly shared by the Saracen's Head Inn and a chemist, it is now occupied by estate agents.

A look up Broad Street with Brown's fish and fruit shop prominent, c.1950.

A mother and her two children spend a quiet afternoon in the churchyard of St Mary's, *c*.1910.

This beautiful house is 'Fernside', seen here in Ashfield (now Archenfield Road) in 1911. Although the house still stands the Victorian canopy has been removed and a small porch built in its place.

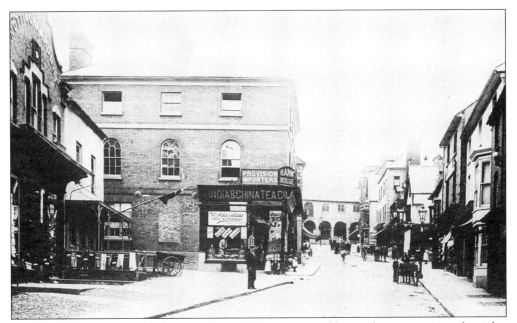

Broad Street as it was in 1905. James Price & Son, renowned house decorators, is on the right. The Ross Coffee House is pictured with its flagpole on the left, next to the India and China Tea shop.

In this picture of Cantilupe Road, you can just see the bell-tower of the Council School through the mist, c.1900.

These cottages in Kyrle Street, which survived until a few years ago, were built for farm-workers. The farmhouse, on the extreme right, was built in 1709. The layout is typical of eighteenth century snobbery, with the workers' front doors on the other side of the building, because the farmer did not wish to see his employees leaving by the same door. One of the many stories attached to these cottages centres around the residents of about 60 years ago. The buildings were known at this time as Menu Row — the occupants being named Cook, Lamb, Bacon and Bullock.

Broad Street at the turn of the century.

Five Ways junction, once an area where children could play.

The junction of Cantilupe Road, Station Road and Smallbrook Road when the Wallace Hall memorial was still standing. Some of the original stone was later used to re-erect it in a truncated form a few yards from the old site.

Alton Street is one of the oldest and most charming streets in the town.

The age of the car was just beginning when these photographs of Broad Street were taken.

The George Hotel before its demolition in 1960, now the site of George Place.

The Hotel wasn't the only building to suffer at the hands of the bulldozers, several adjacent shops were also demolished.

Going, going......

Gone.

Royal Hotel Approach, Ross

The buildings in Palace Pound, as we look down Royal Hotel Approach, are much the same now as when this photo was taken in the early part of this century.

Horses have left their mark on Wilton Road as it curves towards the river. Red Hill looks more manageable for the walker than it does today.

A view of the High Street seventy years ago.

View by the tower, showing the 'Horse Shoe Bend' in the River Wye, *c.*1920.

It is not only the absence of traffic, at what is now the busy Five Ways junction, that makes this view from the early years of the century look so different from today. The two bridges that carried the Ross-Hereford railway have gone, as have nearly all the buldings. Behind the bridge, on the right, you can just see the bell-tower of the Over Ross Mission Room, closed in 1976.

The Valley Hotel with its mock-Tudor front.

The Methodist Church on Edde Cross Street, pictured before and during (below) its demolition. The old red sandstone used for the construction of the Methodist Church in 1867, began to crumble soon after its centenary. The foundation stone for the new building was laid on the same site in 1972.

John Kyrle's Gate at Prospect Gardens, pictured in 1901. In 1700 Kyrle gave the Prospect to the people of the town on a 999 year lease.

The Board Schools (later known as Council Schools) in Cantilupe Road, were opened in 1874 with accommodation for 426 children. The bell-tower, seen in the centre of the picture, was demolished in 1943 and the remainder of the school was razed to the ground in 1968. It was replaced by Ashfield Park School and the county library now stands on this site.

The Swan Hotel, opposite the Valley Hotel, certainly looked the part during its heyday. Now, after several years of standing empty, plans are under way to convert the building into offices for the District Council.

The need for widening Wilton Bridge had not yet arisen, though its time was soon to come following the advent of the car.

The new Stock Market was opened in September of 1871, replacing the long-standing quagmire at Wye Street and Edde Cross Street.

"Royal" Hotel,
ROSS-ON-WYE.

FAMILY AND RESIDENTIAL.
Best Hotel in the Wye Valley.
Stands in Private Grounds overlooking the "Horse Shoe Bend" of the River
- - Every Comfort. Posting. Garage. Petrol. Greases, etc - - -
Send for Illustrated Tariff.

Telegrams, "Royal Hotel. Ross."   Phone, P.O.40

The 'Royal' Hotel stood proud up on the bank of the Wye and can be seen in almost any picture of Ross taken from the river, including the one on the cover of this book.

A closer look at the Royal Hotel, c.1910.

The Chase Hotel pictured in 1911.

Three
The Market House

The Market House in the 1920s

A building that has seen so much come and go over the years and one that has played a large part in the history of the town. The 'Old Man of Ross' has watched the people of Ross go about their daily business for over three centuries. Standing at the top of Broad Street or the Gloucester Road, you can almost experience the sights, sounds, and smells of days gone by. Market traders bustling for position, bellowing their wares at the shoppers with mischievous children playing around the stalls. Built of soft red sandstone, the present Market House was built on the order of the Duchess of Somerset in 1667 and over the years has served as a boys' school, a ballroom, the library, a magistrates' court and the council chamber. Its predecessor, The Booth Hall, stood on part of the existing site and was demolished to make way for the new Market House. Several features of the old wooden building have survived — the balcony rail which faces onto Broad Street and parts of the main staircase.

The Market House in 1954.

The town appears deserted as a lady parks her car on this beautiful summer's morning. If the sign on the Market House is anything to go by, the peace and tranquillity of this scene would not last long, the carnival was only a few days away!

The Market House and High Street photographed in 1920. The motor car pictured on the left-hand side is believed to be the first to be owned locally. It certainly didn't have any problems in parking. Also, notice the solitary gas lamp standing in the middle of the street. When Mr Drew, the lamp-lighter, appeared with his long staff over his shoulder, the children who were playing in the street knew it was time to go home.

The advent of cars, and now buses, gathers pace and a Womens Union group prepares to set off on a day trip to Hereford, c.1930.

The Market House provides a fine setting for the hustle and bustle of market day in the late 1930s.

It is probable that this photograph of the Ross community gathered around the Market House was taken in 1910, on the day that George V was proclaimed King of England following the death of Edward VII.

Four
Public Services and the Military

Captain Alfred Bird (front left), of the Ross United Council fire brigade and his men stand to attention, c.1906.

The spirit of the community during the First World War is shown all over the faces of these members of the Ambulance Nursing Service, c.1943.

Soon after its formation in 1931, Ross St Johns Ambulance Division was winning cups in all parts of the country. This skilful quartet, pictured in 1933, is made up of (from left to right): George Eltome who had much to do with the Division coming into being and was its first secretary, Alan Neno and, on the right, Frank James. The name of the third man is not known.

A Ross contingent of soldiers just before they left for the Boer War in 1899.

The League of Hospital Friends stage a mock operation outside the Market House during a fund-raising event for the Cottage Hospital, c.1910.

Here, Alfred Bird is seen in the centre of this 1910 photograph, together with his men and horse-drawn appliances outside the fire headquarters in St Mary's Street.

The British Legion parading to the 1963 Herefordshire County Rally held at Chase Grounds.

The band of the Staffordshire Regiment leads a march from the Hildersley camp site towards the town centre, *c.*1913.

Sports Day at the Territorial Army camp at Hildersley in 1910, though quite what sport they're playing I really don't know.

The Ross-on-Wye fire brigade of 1900.

A fleet of postal vans seen shortly after the move to new garages on Old Gloucester Road.

A contingent of the Royal Gloucestershire Hussars, possibly on a recruitment drive in the town during the early 1930s, line up their Rolls-Royce armoured cars outside the Market House.

Five

Business as Usual

David Smith's bakery and confectionery at 22, Broad Street in around 1900.

Stephen's Dairy on the High Street in about 1909. It is now the home of Relics & Memories.

Ross jeweller, H.E. Phillips, advertises his wedding rings and decorative talents at the town carnival, *c.*1930.

You wouldn't know from this picture that a fine black and white Tudor facade was hidden beneath the plaster that covered the Man of Ross House when Thomas Matthews had his chemists shop there. Amongst the more expected items in his shop such as cod liver oil and digestive tablets, Matthews also sold cigars, tobacco and even provided a teeth-removal service at 6d each. However, he did not provide an anaesthetic.

Andrews the tailor and hatter in the Market Place kept the gentlemen of Ross stylishly attired as does their successor, Mervyn James, today.

John Kyrle House, the home of the 'Man of Ross' from 1660 until his death in 1724. After his death, the building, which was built in the late sixteenth century, was used as an inn — the Kings Arms. When the inn was closed in 1805 the building was seperated and housed a chemist and a printer. And so it remains almost two hundred years on, though now it is also home to The Ross Gazette. This photograph was taken shortly after the newspaper moved here in 1915, following Mr Jeffries' purchase of the established Powle printing business.

John Kyrle House, pictured through one of the Market House arches. The newsboard leaning against the front of the shop tells of, amongst other things, the funeral of Lord Salisbury, another cup football fiasco and a Gloucester sensation.

Employees at Haig Engineering, c.1960.

Woodville Rubber Company's first factory, built in 1961, provided Ross with a new industry and increased employment.

Lewis's grocery shop in High Street was renowned locally for its home-made pop. It also retained a licence to sell alcohol as it was on the site of the old Swan & Falcon. The licence has now gone but the name Falcon remains in the name of a gift shop, c.1900.

It's a shame that services like the one provided by Webb & Co. are so very rare these days. This butcher, or high class meat purveyor as he was called, would deliver the Sunday roast with a smile and a beautifully decorated bicycle.

A detail of one of the windows at Powle's shop, seen earlier.

The chemists shop in Broad Street retains the name Benjamin to this day, although it has long had proprietors of a different name, c.1900.

Auctioneers and valuers, Dampier & Wigmore, presided over their business at 31, High Street during the early years of this century. Judging by the posters on the window, housing was not the only market they dealt in.

James Price, picture-framer, gilder, glazier and Ross' most prominent house decorator, stands in the doorway of his Broad Street shop (now Woolworths), surrounded by decorations in honour of Queen Victoria's Diamond Jubilee in 1897. To Mr Price's right stands one of the town's characters, George Richards, known locally as 'Rumsher'.

A detail of the children seen in the previous picture outside the shop of house decorator, James Price.

Mr A.Tong, the town confectioner, c.1910.

This traction engine belonged to the Price brothers who owned a small haulage firm in Coughton. Much of their work involved the handling of large amounts of timber, such as the trunck shown, cut down from the nearby forest by hand with a cross-cut saw and transported to the local timber merchant.

CARADOC ..
FRUIT .. ..
PLANTATION
:: ROSS

Telegrams :
'Picts-Cross

Telephone :
31 Ross

CARADOC SCARLET APPLE AT 10 YEARS

An advertising postcard for the local fruit farm.

Six

Horse and Hoof

A morning ride in a donkey cart.

Private transport in the early part of this century was indeed something to be seen. This picture of perfect elegance shows the impressive-looking coachman, William Ford and the wife of Captain Walsh of Wilton, *c.*1905.

The most commonly used mode of transport of the time (apart from walking), was the pony and trap, *c.*1900.

Two ladies pose for the camera before a ride in their pony and trap.

Although traffic through the junction of Broad Street, Gloucester Road and the High Street was minimal at the time of this photograph, a policeman or RAC scout on point duty was a common sight. About 30 years ago the new Chief Constable deemed it to be no longer necessary.

Prior to the construction of the huge roundabout on the M50 at Ross, this was a quiet road junction, with roads going to Ledbury and Newent. The building shown in the picture was the blacksmith's shop which not only later took on the name 'Black House' but gave its name unofficially to the Travellers' Rest pub a few yards along the Ledbury Road. After the opening of the M50, the pub was replaced by a modern roadhouse, which keeps the name Travellers' Rest though occasionally you will still hear locals talk of the Black House roundabout, *c.*1957.

While the roar of traffic through Ross eased, the building of fast roads around the town removed the tranquillity of the countryside. Now at the Wilton junction of the Hereford Road there is a roundabout with an almost unrelentless stream of traffic. This photo of the spot, taken in 1952, shows the once quiet junction.

Not a car in sight outside the Spread Eagle (now the Mill Race) at Walford.

Cycling was still a popular mode of transport at this time, even when the ownership of cars had became widespread. The bridge at Hoarwithy, c.1930.

Cars were becoming more widespread throughout Ross and also in the surroundingvillages. This very smart model is pictured outside the Wormelow Telegraph and Post Office, c.1930.

Seven
The Sporting Life

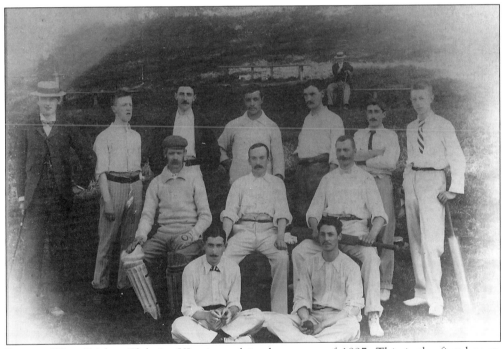

Ross-on-Wye Cricket Club 1st XI, pictured in the season of 1897. This is the first known photograph of a Ross cricket team and was taken before the game became a 'well-to-do' pastime. The first match to be played in Ross, was contested between Hereford and Gloucester, at Wilton Common on Monday August 22nd 1736, and the following year Ross Cricket Club was founded, playing their games at Weir End. On July 7th of 1737, to mark the opening of the new ground, a game was organised between the single men and the married men of Ross. The leading player of the time was Charles Richardson, inventor of the crossbow patent given to the manufacturers, Calclicot. On August 28th 1738, Ross hosted its first county match, between Herefordshire and Gloucestershire. In 1760 the club moved to new grounds at Wilton Common and seven years later, the new and existing Ross-on-Wye Cricket Club was formed.

A Ross cricket team, more than likely of the 'gentry', *c*.1900.

Ross 1st XI, pictured sitting outside the Hereford Cricket Club pavillion, before a league game on June 6th 1925. From left to right, back row: Maxstead, Thomas, Lane, Peachey, Taylor, Wilden. Front row: Ellis, Roff, Meredith, Abbott, West.

Groundsman Reg Preece and player Mr J. Woodward prepare the square for the forthcoming 1932 season at Ross Cricket Club.

Ross 1st XI of 1937. From left to right, back row: C. Downes, Kewley, D. West, C. Peachey, Marmite, Constance. Front row: R. Webb, -?-, R.W.P.Roff, -?-, J. Newton.

Ross Cricket Club 1st XI in 1948. From left to right, back row: Thomas, -?-, -?-, West, Taylor, Ruck, Higton. Front row: Roff, Roff, -?-, -?-, Bailey.

This 1952 team is considered to be one of the best the town has ever produced. From left to right, back row: R. Hicks, R.H. Roff, P. Notley, Sainsbury, L. Wall, E. Sainsbury, R. Bulgin. Front row: D. West, R.W.P. Roff, K. Higton (capt), D. Ruck, H. Ruston, P. Pascoe.

Members of Ross Ladies Gymnasium stop to perform for the camera during a routine practice in 1908.

The Symonds Yat pair just about clinch it on the line from Ross at the Regatta, c.1910.

A foursomes team in action at the Ross Regatta, c.1910.

Walter Scotts School football team pictured in 1922.

Ross United Football Club in their cup-winning season of 1962-63.

When the young lads of Ross returned from the the Second World War as men, the sporting scene had changed quite a bit and they found that their once secure positions in the football team were now filled with a new generation of youthful sportsmen. So Ross United Servicemen Football Club was founded, a team comprising only of those who had served in the forces. As can be seen from the photograph they swept the board, winning almost every trophy on offer, something they continued to do with some regularity for quite a few seasons to come.

Ross-on-Wye Rugby Football Club 1964-65.

Eight

The Life and Death of the Railways

The up platform at Ross Station, c.1900.

The train for Monmouth as it leaves Kerne Bridge station in the early part of this century. The Ross-Monmouth line was opened in August of 1873. The pony and trap in the background belonged to the village store in Goodrich and often travelled down to the station to collect provisions bought in from around the country. After serving the two towns for 86 years, the line was closed in 1959 but the station lives on and now provides a home for the Kerne Bridge Adventure Centre.

In 1891, thirty six years after the opening of the Hereford and Gloucester line, this fine station was built. It saw little change in appearance until its closure in 1959.

A view from the Hereford end of Ross Station.

An 0-6-0 Collet pulling away from the goods shed at Ross station.

The double track shown running along the platform at Holme Lacy did not run parallel for long. Sometimes even before the end of the platform they merged into one. Fortunately there were not many accidents!

Ross station, January 1959. Only nine months before its closure but engine 4107 maintains the tradition of steam-power which was to last until the end.

Ross Station, c.1935.

Ross Station, *c.*1950. Notice the cantilever roofing.

A view of the down platform at Ross Station, *c.*1950.

Symonds Yat Station at the turn of the century. During the summer months, the station would have been crowded with visitors. When the line closed in 1959, the old station was abandoned, though the buildings stood for many years afterwards.

The demolition squad move in on Symonds Yat Station.

Weston-under-Penyard, the last stop before Ross.

The crew of the last Ross to Monmouth train before the closure of passenger services through Ross in October 1959. The engine driver (on the left) is Mr Soules.

A last farewell, as Ross Station feels the heavy hand of the demolition squad.

The dismal scene at Ross Station in the 1960's before demolition.

The tunnel on the Lea Line was the terminus for the trains from Gloucester for several months before the extension to Ross was completed in 1855. Attempts were made to link the Forest of Dean network with the Gloucester line but due to difficulties the line only ever went as far as Drybrook.

The station at Mitcheldean Road was in the nearby village of Lea, and formed part of the Forest of Dean Network. After the unsuccessful attempt to link the network with the main Gloucester line, the station continued to serve its passengers until 1959, when the station waved farewell to the last passenger train as it pulled out towards Gloucester.

The railway at Kerne Bridge.

Nine

The Wye:
Friend and Adversary

The Wye can be enticing and a picture of beauty in the summer, but it can also be an enemy. After many years of flooding, walls were strategically built to keep the water out of the town.

As can be seen from the crowded deck in this picture, the paddlesteamer, Wilton Castle was a popular means of enjoying the delights of the river in the early part of this century. The vessel was built, owned and operated by Henry Dowell, who was also landlord of the Hope and Anchor Inn.

Rarely has the Wye been frozen from bank to bank but the ice was one foot thick in February of 1963. John Coombes photographed his son Adrian and friends walking across the river at Wilton Bridge.

The landing stage and boat house on the Benhall side of the river, possibly, during a Ross regatta in the early 1930s.

Before the construction of Wilton Bridge in the late sixteenth century, the only means of crossing the river was by ford or by ferry. The old ferry landing stage is now marked by a stone cross, c.1920.

Until the recent drainage scheme, Brookend Street was frequently flooded in heavy storms. The street has not changed much since this picture was taken in the mid-1930s. Blakes ironmongers shop (on the left) is today, an entrance to a car park. At the end of the street is the old mill and to the right is Langford's Dining Rooms, once an important social venue for the Ross community.

Today the river really would have to rise to an exceptional height for the flood waters cause a scene like this.

The Oak Meadow did not escape either.

In the mid 1870s, when this picture was taken, the coracle was in use all along the River Wye. It was used for transporting both people and goods as well as for fishing on the stretch of water below the Hope and Anchor. The older man sitting in this coracle is believed to be Sammy Jones, an old local fisherman, who died in 1883 at the grand old age of 93.

Typical English weather! The courts at the local tennis club are flooded during the summer of 1911.

This photograph of the riverside and the upper part of Wye Street was taken in about 1905. The paddle steamer, 'Wilton Castle' is tied to its moorings and the owner, Henry Dowell, stands proudly by the funnel.